Teaching Christian Children About
Feeling Angry

Written by:
Corine Hyman

Illustrated by:
Almar Denso

Hello, my name is Tayniesha. My friends and family call me Tay.

Dear Reader,

This book was created out of my desire to teach children and adults that the Bible contains answers for all of life's questions. I am praying that this book is a blessing to you. In this book, you will learn that God gave you all your feelings, even anger. Because God gave you all your feelings, it is okay to feel angry as long as you do not sin. In this book, you will also learn what the Bible says you should do when you are angry, what to do if someone is angry at you, and what to do about people who are always angry.

To learn more about me or to download free resources for this book, please visit my website www.booksbycorine.com. You can also contact me there. I love hearing from my readers.

As always, please pray for me and know that I am praying for you,
Corine

Teaching Christ's Children
Baltimore, Maryland

www.tccpublishing.com

I live with my mom, brother and cousin. I love my
family, and we get along really well most of the time.

But sometimes they make me angry. Like when my brother teases me, I sometimes feel angry and call him names. Then we both have to go to time out.

Or when my mommy tells me it is time to go home right when my show is getting really, really good ...

I sometimes stomp out of the room. Not only do I have to come back and walk "nicely," but my mom also makes me go to bed early.

If I want to play with the princess doll and my cousin won't let me,

sometimes I feel angry and throw the toy I am playing with. Then I can't play anymore.

Sometimes, I even feel angry at me, like when I lose my shoes. Or I may feel angry without knowing why.

When I get angry, my face turns really, really mean. My heart beats really, really fast. And I ball my hands into a really, really tight fist.

When I get angry, I sometimes say mean things, like, "You are the meanest brother in the whole world." And, sometimes, I even want to hit people.

When I get really, really angry I usually get into really, really big trouble and need a time out.

I get angry so often, my mom decided to help me learn what the Bible says about anger.

My mom tells me that anger is one of the many feelings God gave me, like happy, sad, silly, and scared. She says because God gave me all my feelings, it is okay for me to feel angry.

However, she says the way I let others know I am angry is not okay.

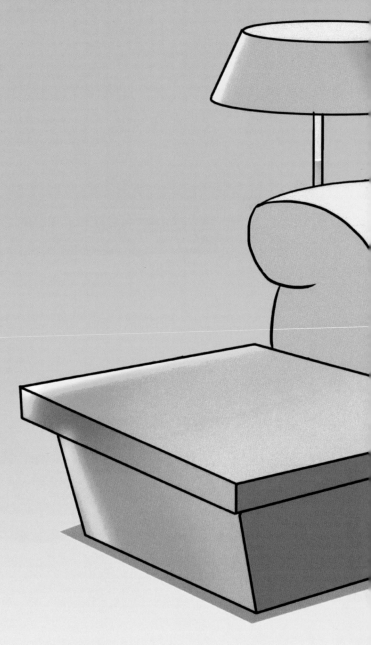

My mom shows me that the Bible tells me it is okay to be angry as long as I do not sin.

✝ When you are angry, do not sin ... (Ephesians 4:26a NCV).

She tells me that God developed my angry feelings so that my body would have a way of telling me that someone did something to me that I do not like. For example ...

Maybe someone told a lie about me,

Broke a promise to me,

Or took something
that belonged to me
without asking first.

She tells me that God also gave me my angry feelings so that I know when I need to protect myself from getting hurt.

At first I did not understand this but then she reminded me of when I played with my neighbor James. He would always hit me and I would become angry. She tells me that this was my body's way of telling me that I needed a break from playing with him.

My mom showed me that the Bible says I should try not to get even with the person I am angry with.

That means I cannot hurt others or things with my words or body when I am angry

No more calling names.

I ask my mom what I should do when I get angry. She tells me the Bible says that I should control my temper.

Some ways I can control my temper are:

Counting slowly to ten;

Saying a prayer;

Taking a deep breath in through my nose and blowing the anger out of me though my mouth;

Using different words to let others know I'm angry...
I'm mad... I'm fuming... I'm irritated... I'm upset;

Listening to my favorite song to calm down;

Or asking a grownup for help.

✝ People with good sense restrain their anger; they earn esteem by overlooking wrongs. (Proverbs 19:11 NLT)

The Bible says I should also try to stop being angry before the day ends.

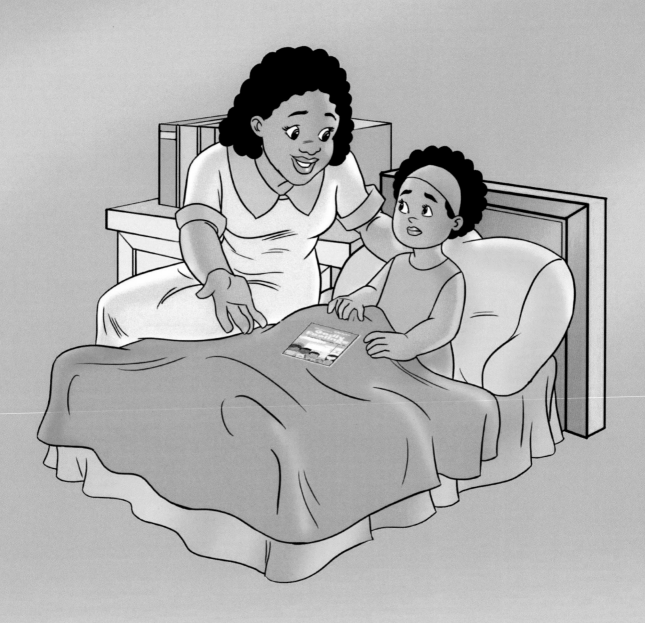

✝ Be angry, and do not sin: do not let the sun go down on your wrath. (Ephesians 4:26 NCV)

I also learned that I should forgive people who make me angry because Jesus forgives me when I do wrong.

 Be kind and loving to each other, and forgive each other just as God forgave you in Christ. (Ephesians 4:32 NCV)

Then I ask my mom what should I do when someone is angry at me, and she tells me I should be quick to listen to why they are angry at me, slow to defend myself, and slow to become angry back.

✝ "Understand this, my dear brothers and sisters: You must all be quick to listen, slow to speak, and slow to get angry." (James 1:19 NLT)

No matter what I do, some people are just angry people. The Bible tells me it is okay if I don't hang around them.

✝ Do not make friends with a hot-tempered person, do not associate with one easily angered, or you may learn their ways and get yourself ensnared." (Proverbs 22:24-25 NLT)

I still get angry when my brother teases me or when we can finally go to the park and it rains. But now I know what God wants me to do about it.

✝ When you are angry, do not sin ... (Ephesians 4:26a NCV)

Scriptures to Memorize as a Family

✝ When you are angry, do not sin … (Ephesians 4:26a New Century Version)

✝ Do not be bitter or angry or mad. Never shout angrily or say things to hurt others. Never do anything evil. (Ephesians 4:31 New Century Version)

✝ People with good sense restrain their anger; they earn esteem by overlooking wrongs. (Proverbs 19:11 New Living Translation)

✝ When you are angry, do not sin, and be sure to stop being angry before the end of the day. (Ephesians 4:26 New Century Version)

✝ Be kind and loving to each other, and forgive each other just as God forgave you in Christ. (Ephesians 4:32 New Century Version)

✝ Understand this, my dear brothers and sisters: You must all be quick to listen, slow to speak, and slow to get angry. (James 1:19 New Living Translation)

✝ Do not make friends with a hot-tempered person, do not associate with one easily angered, or you may learn their ways and get yourself ensnared. (Proverbs 22:24-25 New Living Translation)

Made in the USA
Columbia, SC
17 December 2019